The Best of
The Beatles

Copyright © 1998 Omnibus Press
(A Division of Book Sales Limited)

ISBN: 0-7119-7557-4
Order No: OP 48121

Exclusive Distributors:
Book Sales Limited, 8/9 Frith Street, London W1V 5TZ, UK
Music Sales Pty Limited, 120 Rothschild Avenue, Rosebery, NSW 2018, Australia.

To the Music Trade only:
Music Sales Limited, 8/9 Frith Street, London W1V 5TZ, UK.

A catalogue record for this book is available from the British Library.

Visit Omnibus Press at http://www.omnibuspress.com

OMNIBUS PRESS
LONDON · NEW YORK · PARIS · SYDNEY

Contents

A Day In The Life.

John Lennon and Paul McCartney

Slow 4

I read the news to-day — oh boy
He blew his mind out in — a car
I saw a film to-day — oh boy
I heard the news to-day — oh boy

A - bout a luck - y man who made the grade
He did - n't no - tice that the lights had changed
The Eng - lish arm - y had just won the war
Four thou-sand holes in Black-burn Lan - ca - shire

And though the news — was ra - ther sad
A crowd of peo - ple stood and stared
A crowd of peo - ple turned a - way
And though the holes — were ra - ther small

Well I just had to laugh - augh —
They'd seen his face be - fore —
But I just had to look —
They had to count them all —

I saw the pho - to - graph - aph

No-bo-dy was real-ly sure If he was from the House of Lords —
Hav-ing read the

book I'd love to turn — you — on —

4

Woke up   got   out of bed   Dragged a comb a-cross my head— Found my way down stairs and drank a cup And look-ing up I no-ticed I was late   Found my coat and grabbed my hat — Made the bus in se-conds flat Found my way up-stairs and had a   smoke— And Some-bo-dy spoke and I went in-to a dream.

Coda

Now they know how ma-ny holes it takes to fill the Al-bert Hall.   I'd love to turn _____ you _____ on.

5

A Hard Day's Night.

John Lennon and Paul McCartney

Moderato

1 & 3 It's been a Hard Day's Night _____ And I've been
work all day _____ To get you

work - ing _____ like a dog _____ It's been a
mon - ey _____ to buy you things _____ _____ And it's

Hard Day's Night _____ I should be
worth it just it hear you say _____ You're gon - na

sleep - ing _____ like a log _____ But when I
give me _____ ev' - ry - thing _____ So why I

get home to you _____ I find the things that you do _____ Will make me
love to come home _____ 'Cos when I get you a - lone _____ You know I

feel _____ al - right You know I kay When I'm home
feel _____ o _____

1. C / **2. C**

to ⊕

ev' - ry thing seems _____ to be al - right

It's been A Hard Day's Night, and I've been working like a dog
It's been A Hard Day's Night, I should be sleeping like a log
But when I get home to you I find the things that you do will make me feel alright

You know I work all day to get you money to buy you things
And it's worth it just to hear you say, you're gonna give me ev'rything
So why I love to come home, 'cos when I get you alone you know I feel okay

When I'm home ev'rything seems to be right
When I'm home feeling you holding me tight, tight Yeah.

You know I feel alright, You know I feel alright.

All My Loving.

John Lennon and Paul McCartney

And I Love Her.

John Lennon and Paul McCartney

Gently

I give her all my love — That's all I
She gives me ev-'ry-thing— And ten-der-
Bright are the stars that shine, — Dark is the

do ____ And if you saw my love —
ly ____ The kiss my lov-er brings—
sky ____ I know this love of mine—

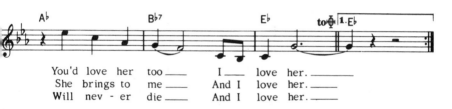

You'd love her too ___ I ___ love her. _____
She brings to me ___ And I love her. _____
Will nev-er die ___ And I love her. _____

— A love like ours — Could nev-er die—

— As long as I _____ have you

near— me.

Coda

D.S. al Coda

9

All You Need Is Love.

John Lennon and Paul McCartney

Moderato

Love   love   love   love   love   love

Love   love   love

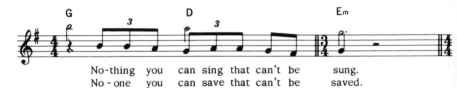

There's no-thing you can do   that can't be   done _____
There's no-thing you can make that can't be   made _____
There's no-thing you can know that is - n't   known_____

No-thing   you   can sing that can't be   sung.
No - one   you   can save that can't be   saved.
No-thing   you   can see that is - n't   shown.

No-thing you can say but you can learn how to   play the   game   It's
No-thing you can do but you can learn how to   be   you in time
No-where you can be that is - n't where___you're meant to   be

ea - sy   All you need is   love

___   All you need is   love. ___

10

All you need is love.— Love— That is all — you need

Love   love   love   Love   love

love   Love   love   love

D.S. al Coda

All you need is love___ All to-gether now   All you need is love

(spoken)

— (Ev-ry-bo-dy)   All you need is   love ___   Love —

Repeat and fade

That is all — you need   That is   all you need   That is
(That is all you need)

11

Back In The U.S.S.R.

John Lennon and Paul McCartney

Brightly

Flew in from Mi - a - mi Beach B. O. A. C.___ Did
Been a - way so long I hard - ly knew the place___ Gee
(*3rd. time piano solo)___
Show me round your snow-peaked mountains way down South ___ Take

- n't get to bed last night ___ On ___ the way the pap-er bag was
_ it's good to be back home ___ Leave ___ it till to-mor-row to un-
(piano solo)___
_ me to your dad-dy's farm ___ Let ___ me hear your ba-la-lai-kas

on my knee___ Man ___ I had a dread-ful flight Did
- pack my case___ Ho - ney dis - con - nect the phone___
(piano solo)___
ring - ing out ___ Come ___ and keep your com - rade warm___

yeah { I'm Back In The U. S. S. R.___ Hey you don't know how luck-y you ar

4th Time **1.** **to ⊕⊕**
_ Boy ___ Back In The U. S. S. R.___
Boy
Boys

2. Ab
Back In The U. S. Back In The U. S. Back In The U. S. S. R.___

Well the U - kraine girls real-ly knock me out__ They leave__ the __West be-hind __ And Mos - cow girls make me sing and shout __ That Geor-gia's al -ways on my mi - mi - mi -mi - mi - mi - mi - mi mind__

Coda

D.S. al *Coda*
D.S. al *Coda*

Well the

Coda

Back In The U. S. S. R.__ Oh yeah

Shouts etc. ad lib.

Blackbird.

John Lennon and Paul McCartney

Slowly

1, 3. Black-bird sing - ing in the dead of night
2. Black-bird sing - ing in the dead of night

Take these broken wings— and learn to fly ——
Take these sunken eyes — and learn to see ——

All your life —— you were on - ly wait-ing for this mo-
All your life —— you were on - ly wait-ing for this mo-

- ment to a - rise—
- ment to be free—

Black - bird— fly ——— Black - bird — fly

In - to the light —— of the dark black

night

Black - bird — fly —

— Black bird — fly —————— In - to the light —

— of the dark black — night

D.S. al ⊕

⊕Coda

You were on - ly — wait-ing for this mo - ment to a - rise—

You were on - ly wait - ing for this mo-ment to — a - rise

15

Can't Buy Me Love.

John Lennon and Paul McCartney

Can't Buy Me Love ___ No no no ___ no.

D.S. al Coda

Coda

___ Can't Buy Me Love ___ Love ___

___ Can't Buy Me Love. ___

Can't Buy Me Love, love, Can't Buy Me Love,
I'll buy you a diamond ring my friend if it makes you feel alright
I'll get you anything my friend if it makes you feel alright
For I don't care too much for money for money Can't Buy Me Love

I'll give you all I've got to give if you say you love me too
I may not have a lot to give but what I've got I'll give to you
For I don't care too much for money for money Can't Buy Me Love
Can't Buy Me Love, Ev'rybody tells me so Can't Buy Me Love, No no no no.

Can't Buy Me Love, love, Can't Buy Me Love
Say you don't need no diamond ring and I'll be satisfied
Tell me that you want those kind of things that money just can't buy
For I don't care too much for money for money Can't Buy Me Love
Can't Buy Me Love, love, Can't Buy Me Love.

Come Together.

John Lennon and Paul McCartney

Slow beat

5th time to ⊕

Sh– Sh– Sh– Sh– (5th time) Ah!

(Me)

D7-10

Here come old flat top he come groov - ing up slow - ly he got
He wear no shoe shine he got toe - jam foot - ball he got
He bag pro-duct-ion he got wal - rus gum - boot he got
He rol - ler coast-er he got ear - ly warn - ing he got

joo joo eye - ball he one ho - ly roll - er he got
fun - ny fin - ger he shoot Co - ca co - la he say
O - no side-board he one spin - al crack-er he got
mud - dy wat - er he one Mo - jo fil - ter he say

A   Am   A   Am

hair down to his knee.___
I know you you know me.___
feet down be - low his knee.___
one and one and one is there.___

G7   1.

Got to be a jok - er he just do what he please.___
One thing I can tell you is you
Hold you in his arm-chair you can
Got to be good look-ing 'cos he's

2.3.4.   Bm   G   A7

got to be free. __
feel his di-sease. __Come to-ge - ther __ right now__ o-ver me__
so hard to see. __

Coda   *Repeat and fade*

⊕   Dm   G   D   Dm   G   D   G   D

Come to-ge - ther. Yeah! Come to-ge - ther.

18

Eight Days A Week.

John Lennon and Paul McCartney

Moderato

Ooh I need your love babe guess you know it's true ____
Love you ev - ry day girl al - ways on my mind ____

Hope you need my love babe just like I need you ____
One thing I can say girl love you all the time ____

Hold me ____ love me ____ hold me ____

love me ____ Ain't got no - thin' but love babe ____

Eight days a week ____

Eight days a week I love ____

____ you ____ Eight days a week is

not e - nough to show I care ____

Eight days a week ____ Eight days a week ____

19

Day Tripper

John Lennon and Paul McCartney

Moderately, with a beat

1. Got a good rea - son for tak - ing the ea - sy way out
2. She's a big tea - ser ___ she took me half ___ the way there
3. Tried ___ to please ___ her ___ she on - ly played ___ one night stand

___ Got a good rea - son for
___ She's a big tea - ser ___
___ Tried to please ___ her ___

tak - ing the ea - sy way out ___ now ⎫ She was a Day _____
She took me half ___ the way there ___ now ⎬ She was a Day _____
she on - ly played one night stands, now. ⎭

Trip - per One way tic - ket, Yeh, ___ It took me
Trip - per Sun - day driv - er, Yeh, ___

so _____ long _____ to find out, ___ and I found

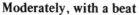

out.

20

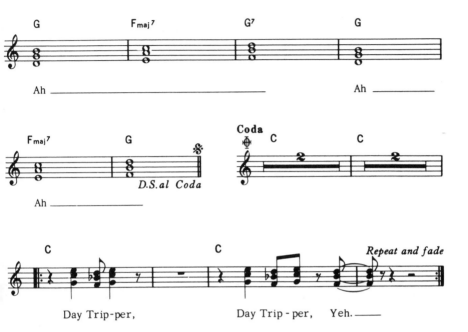

Day Trip-per,   Day Trip-per,   Yeh. ____

Got a good reason for taking the easy way out
Got a good reason for taking the easy way out now
She was a Day Tripper, One way ticket, Yeh,
It took me so long to find out, and I found out.

She's a big teaser she took me half the way there
She's a big teaser she took me half the way there now
She was a Day Tripper, One way ticket, Yeh,
It took me so long to find out, and I found out.

Tried to please her she only played one night stands.
Tried to please her she only played one night stands, now
She was a Day Tripper Sunday driver, Yeh,
It took me so long to find out, and I found out.

     Ah. . . . Ah. . . . Ah. . . .
     Day Tripper, Day Tripper, Yeh. . . . (Repeat and fade)

Drive My Car.

John Lennon and Paul McCartney

Moderately, with a beat

1. Asked a girl what she want-ed to be,___ She said, Ba-by,
2. I told that girl that my pros-pects were good, She said, Ba-by, it's
3. I told that girl I could start right a-way,___ She said, Ba-by, I've got

Can't you see,___ I wan-na be fa-mous, a star of the screen,___ But
un-der-stood,___ Work-ing for pea-nuts is all ve-ry fine,___ But
some-thing to say,___ I got no car and it's break-ing my heart,___ But

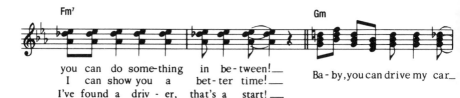

you can do some-thing in be-tween!___
I can show you a bet-ter time!___ Ba-by, you can drive my car___
I've found a driv-er, that's a start!___

___ Yes, I'm gon-na be a star.___

Ba-by you can drive my car,___ and may-be I'll love___ you.

___ you. Beep Beep Mm Beep Beep, Yeh!___

22

Ba-by, you can drive my car.___ Yes, I'm gon-na be a star.

Ba-by, you can drive my car___ and may-be I'll love ___ you.

D.S.

Coda

Repeat and fade

___ you.   Beep Beep Mm Beep Beep, Yeh !___

Asked a girl what she wanted to be
She said, Baby, can't you see,
I wanna be famous, a star of the screen,
But you can do something in between.

Baby, you can drive my car,
Yes, I'm gonna be a star.
Baby, you can drive my car,
And maybe I'll love you.

I told that girl that my prospects were good,
She said, Baby, it's understood,
Working for peanuts is all very fine,
But I can show you a better time.

Baby, you can drive my car,
Yes, I'm gonna be a star.
Baby, you can drive my car,
And maybe I'll love you.

Beep Beep Mm, Beep Beep, Yeh!
Baby, you can drive my car,
Yes, I'm gonna be a star.
Baby, you can drive my car,
And maybe I'll love you.
Beep Beep Mm, Beep Beep, Yeh!

I told that girl I could start right away,
She said, Baby, I've got something to say.
I got no car and it's breaking my heart,
But I've found a driver, that's a start!

Eleanor Rigby.

John Lennon and Paul McCartney

Moderately, with a steady beat

Ah, _____ Look at all ___ the lone - ly peo - ple. ___

E- lea-nor Rig - by picks up the rice ___ in the church.
Fa-ther Mc-ken - zie, writ - ing the words ___ of a ser -
E- lea-nor Rig - by died in the church ___ and was bur -

_____ Where a wed - ding has been ___ Lives in a dream. ___
mon that no - one will hear ___ No- one comes near. ___
ied a long ___ with her name ___ No - bo - dy came. ___

Waits at the win ___ dow, wear-ing the face ___ that she keeps ___
Look at him work - ing, darn - ing his stocks ___ in the night ___
Fa-ther Mc - ken - zie wip - ing the dirt ___ from his hands ___

___ in a jar ___ by the door. ___ Who is it for? ___
___ when there's no - bo - dy there. ___ What does he care? ___
___ as he walks from the grave. ___ No one was saved. ___

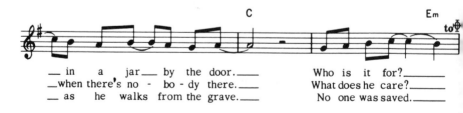

All the lone - ly peo - ple, ___ where do ___ they all ___ come from

All the lone - ly peo - ple, where do __ they all __ be-long __ Ah __ Look at all __ the lone - ly peo - ple. __

D.S. al Coda

(Ah __ Look at all the lone - ly peo-ple)

Coda

All the lone - ly peo - ple, where do __ they all __ come from?

(Ah __ Look at all __ the lone - ly peo -

All the lone - ly peo - ple, where do __

- ple.)

they all __ be __ long? __

25

From Me To You.

John Lennon and Paul McCartney

Medium Tempo with a beat

If there's a - ny - thing that you want If there's

a - ny - thing I can do Just call on me _____ And I'll

send it a - long _____ with love _____ from me _____ to you _____ I've got

ev - 'ry - thing that you want Like a heart __ that's oh so

true Just call on me _____ And I'll send it a - long _____ with love

_____ from me _____ to you _____ I got arms that long to

hold __ you _____ and keep you by my side I got

lips that long to kiss you And keep you sa - tis - fied If there's
a - **ny** -thing that you want If there's a - ny - thing I can do Just
call on me ... And I'll send it a - long with love from me to you.
If there's

If there's anything that you want
If there's anything I can do
Just call on me and I'll send it along
With love from me to you

I've got ev'rything that you want
Like a heart that's oh so true
Just call on me and I'll send it along
With love from me to you

I got arms that long to hold you
And keep you by my side
I got lips that long to kiss you
And keep you satisfied

If there's anything that you want
If there's anything I can do
Just call on me and I'll send it along
With love from me to you

Get Back.

John Lennon and Paul McCartney

32 Bars per minute

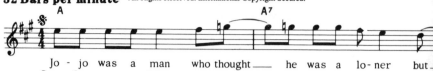

Jo - jo was a man who thought __ he was a lo - ner but __
Sweet Lor - et - ta Mar - tin thought __ she was a wo - man but __

__ he knew it could-nt last _____ Jo - jo left his home in Tuc
__ she was an - o -ther man _____ All __ the girls a-round her say.

- son A - ri - zo - na for __ some Ca - li - for - nia grass
__ she's got it com-ing but __ she gets it while she can

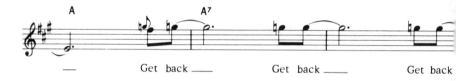

__ Get back __ Get back __ Get back

__ to where you once be-longed _____ Get back __ Get back

__ Get back __ to where you once be-longed _____

Solo 2nd and 3rd times ad lib.

28

Go home! *Take 1st time bar at D.S.*

Get back —   Get back —   (Get) back

— to where you once be-longed —   Get back —   Get back

— (Get) back — to where you once be-longed —

Get back Joe   *D.S.*   Ooh —

(Spoken) Oh!   get back Lor - et - ta   your mother's
2nd Wearing her highheel shoes and her low neck sweater Get on

wait-in' for you   home Loretta Get back — oh get back

Repeat and fade

— Get back — to where you once be-longed —   Get back

29

Girl.

John Lennon and Paul McCartney

1. Is there an - y - bod - y going to list - en to my stor - y,
think of all the times I tried so hard to leave her,
told when she was young that pain would lead to plea - sure,

All a - bout the girl who came to stay, She's the
She will turn to me and start to cry, And she
Did she un - der-stand it when they said, That a

kind of girl you want so much it makes you sor - ry,
prom - is - es the earth to me and I be - lieve her,
man must break his back to earn his day of leis - ure,

Still you don't re - gret a sing - le day.
Af - ter all this time I don't know why. Ah, Girl,____
Will she still be - lieve it when he's dead.

oothss (Breathe in) Girl, Girl.____   2. When I

She's the kind of girl who puts you

30

down, When friends are there, you feel a fool. — (Tu tu tu tu

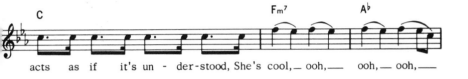

tu tu tu tu tu tu tu tu) When you say she's look-ing good, — She

acts as if it's un - der-stood, She's cool, — ooh, — ooh, — ooh, —

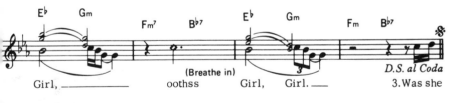

Girl, _____ oothss Girl, Girl. __ 3. Was she

Coda

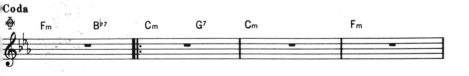

31

Help.

John Lennon and Paul McCartney

Moderato

changed my mind   I've   op - ened   up   the   doors ___
need   you   like   I've   nev - er   done   be - fore ___

Help   me   if   you   can   I'm   feel - ing   down _____

___   And I   do -   ap - pre - ci - ate ___   you   be - ing   round

_____   Help   me   get ___   my

feet   back   on   the   ground _____   Won't you

please   please ___   help ___   me ___

___   Help   me   Help   me ___   oo.

33

Here Comes The Sun.

George Harrison

Moderately Bright

Here Comes The Sun,___ Here Comes The Sun,___

___ (and I say,) "It's all - right"

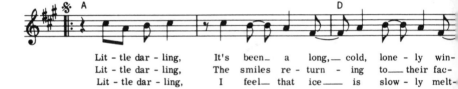

Lit - tle dar - ling, It's been_ a long,__ cold, lone - ly win-
Lit - tle dar - ling, The smiles re - turn - ing to__ their fac-
Lit - tle dar - ling, I feel_ that ice__ is slow - ly melt-

- ter. Lit - tle dar - ling, It feels_ like years
- es. Lit - tle dar - ling, It seems. like years
- ing. Lit - tle dar - ling, It seems. like years

___ since it's __ been here.___
___ since it's __ been here.___
___ since it's __ been clear.__

Here Comes The Sun,

___ Here Comes The Sun,___ (and I say,)

34

"It's all - right,"

Sun, sun,

sun, Here it comes.

comes.

⊕**Coda**

Here Comes— The Sun,——— Here Comes The Sun,—

— It's all - right.

It's all - right.

35

The Fool On The Hill.

John Lennon and Paul McCartney

Hey Jude.

John Lennon and Paul McCartney

Slowly

Hey Jude _____ don't make it bad Take a

sad song__ and make it bet -ter __ Re- mem-ber to let her in - to your

heart Then you can start _____ to make it __ bet - ter__ Hey

1. Jude _____ don't be a - fraid You were made to __ go out and
2. Jude _____ don't let me down You have found her __ now go and

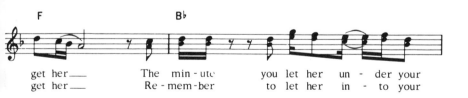

get her__ The min - ute you let her un - der your
get her__ Re - mem-ber to let her in - to your

skin Then you be - gin _____ to make it _____ bet - ter__
heart Then you can start _____ to make it _____ bet - ter__

skin Then you'll be-gin — to make it bet - ter, bet - ter, bet - ter, bet - ter,

bet - ter, bet - ter, Oh da da da da da da da

Da da da da Hey Jude Da da da

da da da da Da da da da Hey Jude.

Repeat and fade

I Saw Her Standing There.

John Lennon and Paul McCartney

Moderato

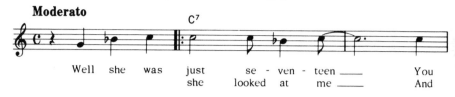

Well she was just se - ven - teen ___ You
she looked at me ___ And

know what I mean ___ And the way she looked was
I, I could see ___ That be - fore too long ___ I'd

way be - yond com - pare ___ So
fall in love with her ___

how could I dance ___ with an - o - ther ___
She would -n't dance ___ with an - o - ther ___

Oh ___ when I saw her stand - ing there.
Oh ___ when I saw her stand - ing there.

Well   Well my heart went boom when I

cross'd that   room   And   I   held   her   hand   in

mine _____ Oh   we   danced

____ through   the   night ____   And   we   held   each   o - ther   tight_

____   And   be - fore   too   long ____   I   fell   in   love   with

her _____ Now   I'll   ne - ver   dance____

____   with   an - o - ther ____   Oh ____ when   I   saw   her

stand - ing   there. ____   Since   I   there. ____

41

I Feel Fine.

John Lennon and Paul McCartney

Moderato Beat

Ba - by's good to me ____ you know ____ She's hap -
Ba - by says she's mine ____ you know ____ She tells
- by buys her things ____ you know ____ He buys

- - py as can be ____ you know ____ She said ____ so
— me all the time ____ you know ____ She said ____ so
— her dia -mond rings ____ you know ____ She said ____ so

I'm in love ____ with her ____ and I ____ feel ____ fine.
I'm in love ____ with her ____ and I ____ feel ____ fine.
She's in love ____ with me ____ and I ____ feel ____ fine.

I'm so glad that

she's my lit - tle girl ____ She's so glad she's

tell -ing all the world. ____ That her ba -

She's in love ____ with me ____ and I ____ feel ____ fine. ____

42

I Wanna Be Your Man.

John Lennon and Paul McCartney

43

I Want To Hold Your Hand.

John Lennon and Paul McCartney

you ___ got that some - thing I think you'll un - der - stand when

I ___ say that some- - thing I wan-na hold your hand___

to Coda ✦

I wan-na hold your hand _____ I wan-na hold your

hand And when I touch you I feel hap-py___ in - side___

___ It's such a feel - ing that my love I can't hide

___ I can't hide___ I can't hide _____ yeh

✤
Coda

hand I wan-na hold your hand___

45

Lady Madonna.

John Lennon and Paul McCartney

Moderately (with a beat)

La - dy   Ma-don-na —   child - ren   at   your   feet

Won - der   how   you   man - age   to   make —   ends   meet —

Who   finds —   the   mon - ey   when   you   pay   the   rent —

Did   you   think   that   mon - ey   was —   hea - ven   sent —

Fri - day   night —   ar - rives —   with out —   a   suit - case
Tues - day   af - ter-noon —   is   nev - er   end - ing

Sun - day morn - ing   creep   in   like   a   nun —
Wedn's - day morn - ing   pa - pers   did - n't   come —

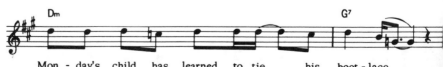

Mon - day's   child   has   learned   to   tie —   his   boot - lace —
Thurs - day   night   your   stock - ings need - ed   mend - ing —

46

See how they'll run   La - dy Ma - don - na

Ba - by at your breast   Won - der how you man - aged to feed
Ly - ing on the bed   Lis - ten to the mu - sic play - ing
Child - ren at your feet   Won - der how you man - age to make

Solo

the rest —
in your head —

ends meet

Norwegian Wood.

John Lennon and Paul McCartney

I once had a girl, or should I say she once had me;

She showed me her room, is-n't it good Nor-we-gian Wood. She

asked me to stay and she told me to sit an-y-where, So
told me she worked in the morn-ing and start-ed to laugh, I

I looked a-round and I no-ticed there was-n't a chair.
told her I did-n't and crawled off to sleep in the bath.

I sat on a rug bi-ding my time, drink-ing her wine,
And when I a-woke I was a-lone, this bird had flown,

We talked un-til two and then she said "It's time for bed."
So I lit a fire, Is-n't it good Nor-we-gian Wood.

D.S. al Coda

2. She

48

I'll Follow The Sun.

John Lennon and Paul McCartney

Moderato

One day — you'll look — to see I've gone —
Some day — you'll know — I was the one —

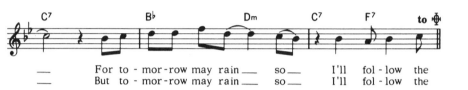

— For to - mor-row may rain — so — I'll fol - low the
— But to - mor-row may rain — so — I'll fol - low the

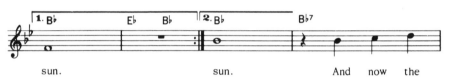

sun.   sun.   And now the

time has come — and so my love — I must go —

And though I lose a friend — In the end — you will know —

— Oh, _____   sun. _____

49

Let It Be.

John Lennon and Paul McCartney

Slow tempo (16 bars per minute)

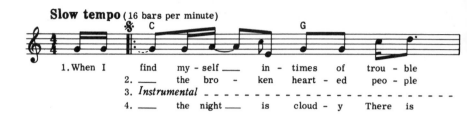

1. When I find my - self ____ in - times of trou - ble
2. ____ the bro - ken heart - ed peo - ple
3. *Instrumental* _
4. ____ the night ____ is cloud - y There is

Moth - er Ma - ry comes to me
Liv - ing in ____ the world a - gree
still a light ____ that shines on me

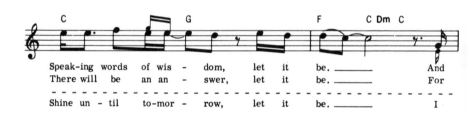

Speak-ing words of wis - dom, let it be. ____ And
There will be an an - swer, let it be. ____ For
Shine un - til to-mor - row, let it be. ____ I

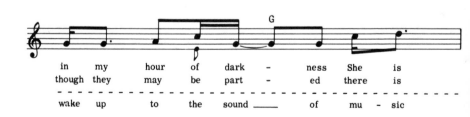

in my hour of dark - ness She is
though they may be part - ed there is
wake up to the sound ____ of mu - sic

stand - ing right in front ____ of me ____
still a chance that they ____ will see ____
Moth - er Ma - ry comes ____ to me ____

50

Love Me Do.

John Lennon and Paul McCartney

Moderato

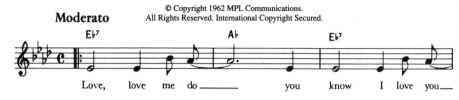

Love, love me do _____ you know I love you _____

_____ I'll al - ways be true _____ So

please _____ love me

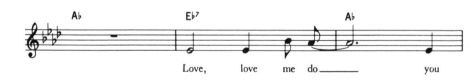

do _____ Wo ho _____ love me do _____

Love, love me do _____ you

know I love you _____ I'll al - ways be true _____

So please _____

52

love me do ___ Wo ho ___

love me do ___ Some - one to

love some - bo - dy new ___ Some - one to

love some - one like you ___ Love, love me do ___

___ you know I love you ___ I'll al - ways be true ___

___ So please ___ love me

do ___ Wo ho ___ love me do. ___

Lucy In The Sky With Diamonds.

John Lennon and Paul McCartney

Pic - ture your - self in a boat on a riv - er with
Fol - low her down to a bridge by a fount - ain where
pic - ture your - self on a train in a sta - tion with

tan - ger - ine trees____ and mar - ma - lade skies
rock - ing horse peo - ple eat marsh-mal - low pies
plast - i - cine port - ers with look - ing - glass ties

Some - bo - dy calls you, you an - swer quite
Ev' - ry - one smiles as you drift past the
Sud - den - ly some - one is there at the

slow - ly a girl with kal - eid - o - scope eyes.____
flow - ers that grow so in - cred - ib - ly high.____
turn - stile the girl with kal - eid - o - scope eyes.____

Cel - lo - phane
News - pa - per

flow - ers of yel - low and green tow - er - ing
tax - is ap - pear on the shore wait - ing to

Maxwell's Silver Hammer.

John Lennon and Paul McCartney

about 40 bars per minute

Joan was quiz - zi - cal stud - ied pat - a - phys - i - cal
Back in school a - gain Max - well plays the fool a - gain
P. C. thir - ty - one said we've caught a dir - ty one

sci - ence in the home ____ Late nights all a - lone
teach - er gets an-noyed ____ Wish - ing to a - void _
Max - well stands a - lone ____ Paint - ing tes - ti - mo -

____ with a test - tube oh oh oh oh ____
____ an un-pleas - ant sce - ee - ee - ene ____
- ni - al pic - tures oh oh oh oh ____

Max - well Ed - i - son ma - jor-ing in me - di - cine
She tells Max to stay when the class has gone a - way
Rose and Val - er - ie scream - ing from the gal - le - ry

calls her on the phone __ Can I take you out __
so he waits be - hind __ Writ - ing fif - ty times __
say he must go free __ The judge does not a - gree _

____ to the pic - tures Jo - oh ho - oan ____ But
____ I must not __ be so oh ho - oan ____ But
____ and he tells __ them so oh ho - oan ____ But

56

as   she's   get - ting   read - y   to   go ____   a
when she   turns her   back ____   on   the   boy ____   he
as   the   words are leav - ing his   lips ____   a

knock comes on   the   door ____   Bang   bang Max - well's
creeps up   from be - hind ____   Bang   bang Max - well's
noise comes from be - hind ____   Bang   bang Max - well's

sil - ver ham - mer came   down up - on her   head ____
sil - ver ham - mer came   down up - on her   head ____
sil - ver ham - mer came   down up - on her   head ____

Bang   bang   Max - well's   sil - ver ham - mer made
Bang   bang   Max - well's   sil - ver ham - mer made
Bang   bang   Max - well's   sil - ver ham - mer made

sure   that   she was   dead. ____

sure   that   she was   dead. ____

57

sure that he was dead. ___

Sil - ver ham - mer man. _____

Yesterday.

John Lennon and Paul McCartney

Moderato (Gently)

Yes-ter-day all my troub-les seemed so far a-way
Sud-den-ly I'm not half the man I used to be
Yes-ter-day love was such an eas - y game to play

Now it looks as though they're here to stay Oh I be-lieve__ in
There's a sha-dow hang-ing ov-er me Oh yes-ter-day__ came
Now I need a place to hide a-way Oh I be-lieve__ in

yes - ter-day__ Why she had to go I don't
sud - den-ly __

know she would-n't say _____ I said

some - thing wrong now I long for yes - ter - day _____

D.S.

Coda

yes - ter-day__ Mm mm mm mm mm mm mm__

59

Michelle.

John Lennon and Paul McCartney

Mich - elle ma belle These are words that go to - geth - er

well My Mich-elle___ Mich - elle ma belle

Sont les mots qui vont tres bien en - semble tres bien en - semble I

love you I love you I love you That's all I want to say
need to I need to I need to I need to make you see
want you I want you I want you I think you know by now

— Un - til I find a way___ I will
— Oh what you mean to me ___ Un -
— I'll get to you some how___ Un -

say the on - ly words I know that you'll un - der - stand
til I do I'm hop - ing you will know what I mean
til I do I'm tell - ing you so you'll un - der - stand

I love you ___ I

60

Coda

F	B♭m7	E♭6	D°	G7-9

Mich - elle   ma   belle   sont - les mots qui   vont tres bien en -

C	G7 _3_	C _3_	Fm	C7

semble   tres bien en - semble   I   will   say   the   on - ly

Fm7	B♭	Fm	B♭m	C7	Fm C7

words   I   know   that   you'll   un - der - stand   My   Mich -

repeat
1st Fine Only F(maj) B♭m   E♭7   D°   C   B°   C7   *& fade*

elle.

Michelle ma belle
These are words that go together well my Michelle
Michelle ma belle
Sont les mots qui vont tres bien ensemble tres bien ensemble

I love you, I love you, I love you
That's all I want to say, until I find a way
I will say the only words I know that you'll understand

Michelle ma belle
Sont les mots qui vont tres bien ensemble tres bien ensemble
I need to, I need to, I need to,
I need to make you see, Oh what you mean to me
Until I do I'm hoping you will know what I mean I love you,

I want you, I want you, I want you,
I think you know by now, I'll get to you somehow
Until I do I'm telling you so you'll understand

Michelle ma belle
Sont les mots qui vont tres bien ensemble tres bien ensemble
I will say the only words I know that you'll understand my Michelle.

Nowhere Man.

John Lennon and Paul McCartney

He's a real No - where Man, sit - ting in __ his
Does - n't have a point of view, knows not where __ he's
He's as blind as he can be, just sees what __ he
Does - n't have a point of view, knows not where __ he's
He's a real No - where Man, sit - ting in __ his

No - where Land Mak - ing all __ his No - where plans __ for
go - ing to. Is - n't he __ a bit like you __ and
wants to see. No - where Man __ can you see me __ at
go - ing to. Is - n't he __ a bit like you __ and
No - where Land Mak - ing all __ his No - where plans __ for

no - bod - y.
me ? _____
all ? _____
me ? _____
no - bod - y.

No - where Man __ please
No - where Man __ don't
No - where Man __ please

lis - ten, __ you don't know __ what __ you're mis - sing, __ No - where Man
wor - ry, __ take your time _____ don't hur - ry, __ leave it all.
lis - ten, __ you don't know __ what __ you're mis - sing, __ No - where Man

— The world _____ is at your com - mand.
— Till some - bod - y else __ lends you a hand.
— The world _____ is at your com - mand.

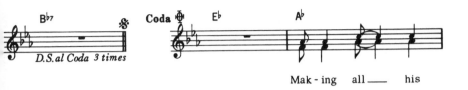

D.S. al Coda *3 times*

Mak - ing all — his

No-where plans — for no - bod - y.

Mak-ing all — his No-where plans — for no-bod-y.

Ob-La-Di, Ob-La-Da

John Lennon and Paul McCartney

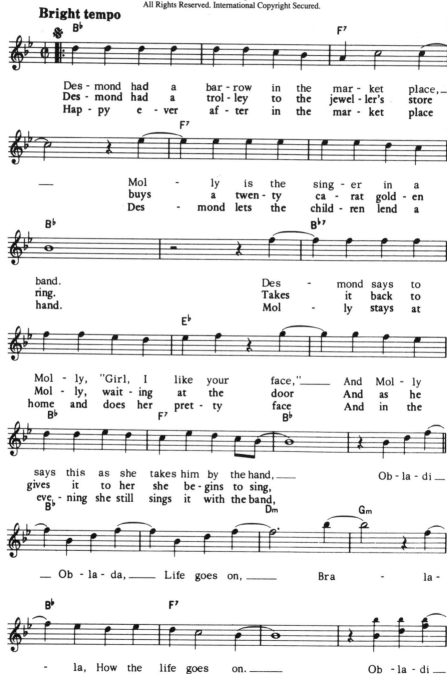

Ob - la - da, ___ Life goes on ___ Bra - la -

- la, How the life goes on. ___

In a cou-ple of years they have built a home ___

___ sweet home. ___

With a cou-ple of kids run - ning in the yard ___

___ Of Des-mond and Mol - ly Jones. ___

D.S. al Coda

Coda

on, And if you want some fun ___

Take Ob - la di - bla - da.

65

Paperback Writer.

John Lennon and Paul McCartney

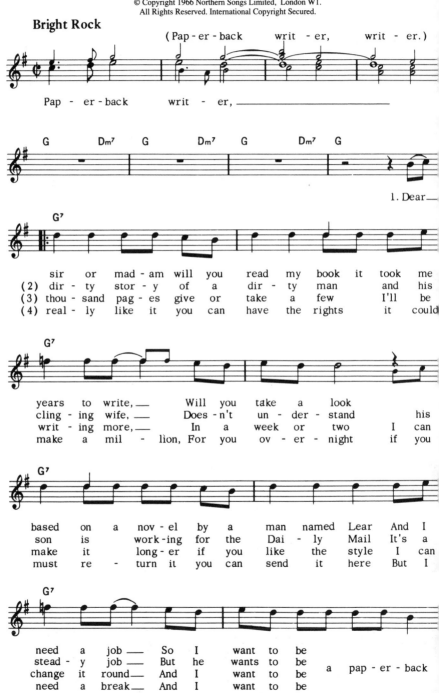

writ - er,   Pap-er-back writ - er._____

1.   **2.**   (Pap - er-back

___ 2. It's a ___ Pap - er-back writ - er.___

writ - er.)

         3.   **4.**

3. It's a ___ 4. If you ___

(Pap - er-back writ - er, writ - er.)

Pap - er-back writ - er._____

(Pap-er-back writ - er.) *Repeat and fade*

Pap - er-back writ - er._____

Penny Lane.

John Lennon and Paul McCartney

Moderate Tempo

In Pen-ny Lane— there is a bar-ber showing pho - to-graphs of ev'ry head
cor-ner is a bank - er with a mo - tor car the lit-tle chil
the bar-ber shavesan-oth-er cus - to-mer we see the ban

— he's had the plea-sure to — know — And all the
- ren laugh at him be -hind his back — And the
- er sit - ting wait - ing for a trim — And then the

peo - ple that come and go — stop and say —"hel -lo"
bank - er nev-er wears a mack— in the pour - ing rain
fire - man rush-es in — from the pour - ing rain

1.   **2. Eb**

On the
Ve-ry strange— Pen- ny Lane —— } is in my ears
Ve-ry strange— Pen- ny Lane —— }

— and in my eyes ——

There be - neath the blue —— sub- ur-ban skies —— I sit, and
—— A **full** of fish —— and fin-ger pies —— in sum-mer
There be - neath the blue —— sub- ur-ban skies—— I sit, and

68

Please Please Me.

John Lennon and Paul McCartney

Moderato (with a beat)

1. Last night I said these words to my _____ girl
2. You don't need me to show the way _____ love

I know you ne - ver e - ven
Why do I al - ways have to

try _____ girl
say _____ love

Come on, come on, come

on, come on, Please Please me Oh Yeh like I please

you.

I don't want to sound com-plaining

But you know there's al - ways rain in my _____ heart.

I do all the pleas-ing with you It's so hard to rea-son with

you. Oh yeh why do you make me blue.

70

Last night I said these words to my _____ girl.

I know you ne - ver e - ven

try _____ girl   Come on,   come on,   come

on,   come on,   Please please me oh yeh like I please

you. _____

Last night I said these words to my girl
I know you never even try girl
Come on, come on, come on, come on,
Please Please Me, oh yeh, like I please you.

You don't need me to show the way love
Why do I always have to say love
Come on, come on, come on, come on,
Please Please Me, oh yeh, like I please you.

I don't want to sound complaining
But you know there's always rain in my heart.
I do all the pleasing with you
It's so hard to reason with you.
Oh yeh, why do you make me blue.

Last night I said these words to my girl.
I know you never even try girl,
Come on, come on, come on, come on,
Please Please Me, oh yeh, like I please you.

Revolution.

John Lennon and Paul McCartney

Moderate tempo

1. You say you want a re-vo-lu-tion _____ Well _____
(2) say you got a real so-lu-tion _____ Well _____
(3) say you'll change the con-sti-tu-tion _____ Well _____

_____ you know _____ we all want _____ to change the
_____ you know _____ we'd all love _____ to see the plan _____
_____ you know _____ we all want _____ to change your

world You tell me that it's e-vo-lu
— You ask me for a con-tri-bu
head You tell me it's the in-sti-tu

- tion _____ Well _____ you know _____ We all want _____
- tion _____ Well _____ you know _____ We're _ do -
- tion _____ Well _____ you know _____ You bet-ter

_ to change the world. _____
- ing what we can. _____
free your mind in - stead. _____

But when you talk a - bout de - struc-tion _____
But when you want mo-ney for peo-ple with minds that hate _____
But if you go car-ry -ing pic-tures of Chair-man Mao _____

72

Don't you know that you can count me out.＿
All I can tell you is bro-ther you have to wait.＿
You ain't going to make it with an - y - one an - y - how.＿

Don't you know it's gon-na be ＿＿ al - right

＿ Al - right ＿＿＿

Al - right ＿＿

2. You
3. You

Al - right ＿＿ Al - right ＿＿＿ Al - right＿

＿ Al - right ＿＿ Al - right ＿＿＿ Al - right

＿ Al - right ＿＿ Al - right. ＿＿＿

73

With A Little Help From My Friends.

John Lennon and Paul McCartney

Moderato

What would you do — if I sang — out of tune — would you stand
What do I do — when my love — is a - way — (does it wor -
Would you be-lieve — in a love — at first sight — yes I'm cer -

— up and walk — out on me — Lend me your ears and I'll sing
— ry you to be — a - lone?) How do I feel — by the end
— tain that it happens all the time (What do you see — when you turn

— you a song — and I'll try — not to sing — out of key —
— of the day — (are you sad — be-cause you're — on your own —
— out the light?) I can't tell — you but I know — it's mine —

— Oh } I get by — with a lit-tle help — from my friends
— No } I get by — with a lit-tle help — from my friends
— Oh }

— Mm, I get high — with a lit-tle help — from my friends

— { Mm, I'm gon-na try } — with a lit-tle help — from my friends
  { Oh, I'm gon-na try }

— with a lit-tle help— from my friends— Yes, I get by—

—with a lit-tle help—from my friends,—with a lit-tle help—from my friends

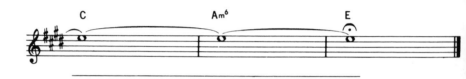

Yellow Submarine.

John Lennon and Paul McCartney

March Tempo

In the town — where I was born Lived a man — who sailed to

sea And he told — us of his life In the

land — of sub - ma - rines. So we sailed — on to the

sun Till we found — the sea of green And we

lived — be neath the waves in our Yel - low Sub - ma -

rine. We all live in a Yel - low Sub - ma - rine,

Yel - low Sub-ma-rine, Yel - low Sub-ma-rine, We all live in a

D

Yel - low Sub - ma - rine, Yel - low Sub - ma - rine, to ⊕

G   D   C

Yel - low Sub - ma - rine.   And our friends   are all   on -
                             As we   live   a life of

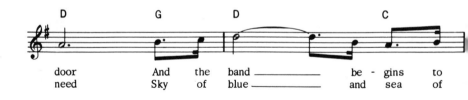

G   Em   Am   Cmaj⁷

'board   Ma - ny   more of them   live   next
ease   Ev - 'ry one   of us   has   all   we

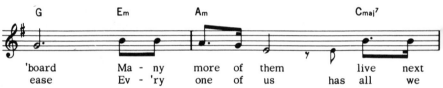

D   G   D   C

door   And the   band _____   be - gins to
need   Sky of   blue _____   and   sea of

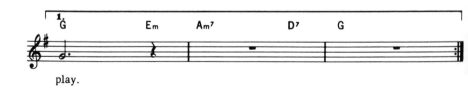

1.
G   Em   Am⁷   D⁷   G

play.

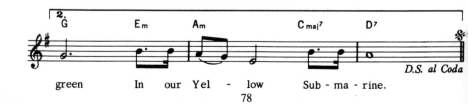

2.
G   Em   Am   Cmaj⁷   D⁷   𝄋

                                          D.S. al Coda

green   In   our Yel - low   Sub - ma - rine.

78

ade 2nd time

Coda

Yel -low Sub-ma-rine, We all live in a Yel - low Sub-ma-rine,

Yel - low Sub - ma - rine, Yel - low Sub - ma - rine,

We all live in a Yel-low Sub-ma-rine, Yel - low Sub-ma-rine.

In the town where I was born lived a man who sailed to sea
And he told us of his life, in the land of submarines.
So we sailed on to the sun, till we found the sea of green
And we lived beneath the waves in our Yellow Submarine.

We all live in a Yellow Submarine, Yellow Submarine,
Yellow Submarine, we all live in a Yellow Submarine,
Yellow Submarine, Yellow Submarine.
And our friends are all aboard
Many more of them live next door
And the band begins to play.

We all live in a Yellow Submarine, Yellow Submarine,
Yellow Submarine, we all live in a Yellow Submarine,
Yellow Submarine, Yellow Submarine.
As we live a life of ease,
Ev'ry one of us has all we need
Sky of blue and sea of green
In our Yellow Submarine.

We all live in a Yellow Submarine, Yellow Submarine,
Yellow Submarine, we all live in a Yellow Submarine,
Yellow Submarine, we all live in a Yellow Submarine
Yellow Submarine, Yellow Submarine,
We all live in a Yellow Submarine, Yellow Submarine.

Sgt. Pepper's Lonely Hearts Club Band.

John Lennon and Paul McCartney

Slow 4

It was twen-ty years a-go to-day _____ that ser-geant
real-ly want to stop the show_____ but I

Pep-per taught the band to play ___ They've been
thought ___ you might like to know ___ That the

go-ing in and out of style ___ but they're
sing-er's going to sing a song ___ and he

gua-ran-teed to raise a smile ___ So
wants you all to sing a-long ___ So

may I in-tro-duce to you ___ the
may I in-tro-duce to you ___ the

act you've known for all these years ___
one and on-ly Bil-ly Shears ___

Ser-geant Pep-per's Lone-ly Hearts Club Band ____

We're

Ser - geant Pep - per's Lone - ly Hearts ____ Club Band ____ We

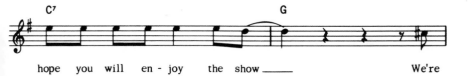

hope you will en - joy the show ____ We're

Ser - geant Pep - per's Lone - ly Hearts ____ Club Band ____ Sit

back and let the eve - ning go _____ Ser -

____ geant Pep-per's Lone - ly Ser - geant Pep-per's Lone - ly Ser -

__ geant Pep - per's Lone - ly Hearts __ Club Band __ It's

won - der - ful to be here it's cer - tain - ly a thrill You're

such a love - ly au - di - ence we'd like to take you home with us we'd

love to take you home I don't

D.S. al Coda

You've Got To Hide Your Love Away.

John Lennon and Paul McCartney

1. Here I stand with head in hand
2. Ev - 'ry - where peop - le stare
3. How can I ev - en try
4. How could she say to me

turn my face to the wall / If she's gone I can't go on
each and ev - 'ry day / I can see them laugh at me
I can nev - er win / Hear - ing them see - ing them
love will find a way / Gath - er round all you clowns

feel - ing two foot small
and I hear them say.
in the state I'm in
let me hear you say

Hey you've got to hide your love a - way.

Hey you've got to hide you love a - way.

4th time to coda

D.S. al Coda

Coda

83

She Loves You.

John Lennon and Paul McCartney

Moderato

She loves you yeh, yeh, yeh, ___ She loves you yeh, yeh, yeh, ___ She

loves you yeh, yeh, yeh, ___ yeh !!! ___ You

think you've lost your love, ___ Well I saw her yes - ter - day-yi - yay, It's
said you hurt her so, ___ ___ She al - most lost her mind, ___ And
know it's up to you, ___ ___ I think it's on - ly fair ___ ___

you she's think - ing of ___ And she told me what to sa - yi - yay. She says she
now she says she knows ___ You're not the hurt - ing kind. ___ She says she
Pride can hurt you too ___ A - pol - o - gize to her. ___ Be - cause she

loves you and you know that can't be bad, ___ ___ Yes, she

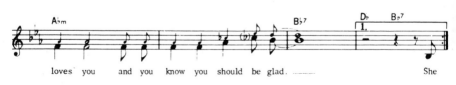

loves you and you know you should be glad. ___ She

Oo She loves you yeh, yeh, yeh, ___ She loves you yeh,

yeh, yeh,— And with a love like that you know you should be glad.

You

With a love like that you

know you should—— be glad,———— Yeh

yeh, veh,—— veh, veh, veh,— veh.————

She Loves You yeh, yeh, yeh, She Loves You yeh, yeh, yeh,
She Loves You yeh, yeh, yeh, yeh!!!

You think you've lost your love, well I saw her yesterday-yi-yay,
It's you she's thinking of and she told me what to sayiyay.
She says she loves you and you know that can't be bad,
Yes, she loves you and you know you should be glad.

She said you hurt her so, she almost lost her mind,
And now she says she knows, you're not the hurting kind,
She says she loves you and you know that can't be bad,
Yes, she loves you and you know you should be glad,.

Oo, She Loves You yeh, yeh, yeh, She Loves You yeh, yeh, yeh,
And with a love like that you know you should be glad.

You know it's up to you, I think it's only fair,
Pride can hurt you too, apologize to her.
Because she loves you and you know that can't be bad,
Yes, she loves you and you know you should be glad.

Oo, She Loves You yeh, yeh, yeh, She Loves You yeh, yeh, yeh,
And with a love like that you know you should be glad.
With a love like that you know you should be glad,
Yeh, yeh, yeh, yeh, yeh, yeh, yeh.

85

Strawberry Fields Forever.

John Lennon and Paul McCartney

Let me take you down___ 'cos I'm go - ing to

Straw - ber - ry Fields   Noth - ing   is real

and noth-ing to get hung a-bout___   Straw-ber-ry Fields For -

ev -er___   Liv- ing   is ea - sy   with eyes   closed

Mis-un-der-stand-ing all you see   It's get-ting hard to be some-

one but it all_works_out   It doesn't mat-ter much to_ me

Let me   take you down___ 'cos I'm   go - ing to

Straw-ber-ry Fields   Noth-ing is real   and noth-ing to get.

hung a-bout,____ Straw-ber-ry Fields__ For - ev-er.____

1. No-one I think is in my tree____
2. Al - ways no some - times think it's me

I mean it must be high or low _____
But you know I know **and** it's a dream _____

That is you can't you know tune in **but** it's all ____ right
I think I know **of thee ah,** yes **but** it's all ____ wrong

That is I think it's not too__ bad.
That is I think I dis - a - gree.

Let me

⊕ **Coda**

- ev-er.____ Straw-ber - ry Fields_ For - ev-er,____

Straw-ber - ry Fields__ For - ev - er.____

87

Ticket To Ride.

John Lennon and Paul McCartney

Moderato

1. I think I'm gon - na be sad, _____ I think it's to - day.
(2. She) said that liv - ing with me _____ is bring - ing her down.

_____ Yeh, _____ The girl that's driv - ing me mad _
_____ Yeh, _____ For she would nev - er be free _

___ is go - ing a - way, ___
___ when I was a - round. ___ She's got a tick - et to ride

_____ She's got a tick - et to ri - hi - hide. ___

She's got a tick - et to ride, _____ but she don't care. _____

2. She I don't know why she's rid - ing so high _

She ought to think right. She ought to do right by

me. Be - fore she gets to say - ing good-bye. _____ She ought to

think twice. She ought to do right by me. She

Coda

Eb   Eb   **Repeat and Fade Out**

My   ba - by don't   care.   My   ba - by don't

I think I'm gonna be sad, I think it's today yeh,
The girl that's driving me mad is going away,
She's got a ticket to ride, she's got a ticket to ri-hi-hide.
She's got a ticket to ride, but she don't care.

She said that living with me is bringing her down, yeh,
For she would never be free when I was around.
She's got a ticket to ride, she's got a ticket to ri-hi-hide.
She's got a ticket to ride, but she don't care.

I don't know why she's riding so high,
She ought to think twice, she ought to do right by me.
Before she gets to saying goodbye.
She ought to think twice, she ought to do right by me.

My baby don't care, My baby don't care. . . . .

89

We Can Work It Out.

John Lennon and Paul McCartney

Moderato

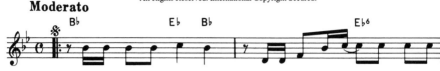

Try to see it my way, do I have to keep— on talk-ing
Think of what you're say - ing; you can get it wrong— and still you
Try to see it my way; on - ly time will tell — if I am

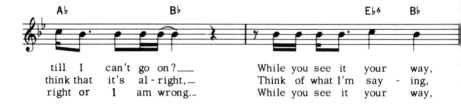

till I can't go on?__ While you see it your way,
think that it's al - right,— Think of what I'm say - ing,
right or I am wrong._ While you see it your way,

run the risk of know - ing that our love may soon be gone.___
we can work it out __ and get it straight, or say goodnight.___
there's a chance that we __ may fall a - part be-fore too long. ___

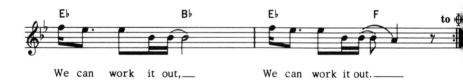

We can work it out,__ We can work it out.___

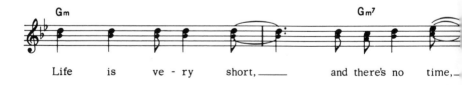

Life is ve - ry short, ___ and there's no time,_

_____ for fus - sing and

90

fight - ing my friend. I have al-ways thought

that it's a crime, _____ So I will

ask you once a - gain.

D.S. al Coda

Coda

Try to see it my way,
Do I have to keep on talking till I can't go on?
While you see it your way,
Run the risk of knowing that our love may soon be gone.
We can work it out, we can work it out.

Think of what you're saying;
You can get it wrong and still you think that it's alright,
Think of what I'm saying,
We can work it out and get it straight or say goodnight.
We can work it out, we can work it out.

Life is very short and there's no time,
For fussing and fighting my friend
I have always thought that it's a crime.
So I will ask you once again.

Try to see it my way;
Only time will tell if I am right or I am wrong.
While you see it your way,
There's a chance that we may fall apart before too long.
We can work it out, we can work it out.

When I'm Sixty Four.

John Lennon and Paul McCartney

Medium tempo

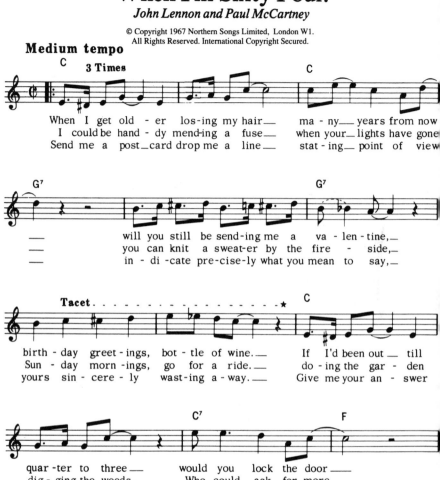

When I get old - er los-ing my hair — ma - ny — years from now
I could be hand - dy mend-ing a fuse — when your — lights have gone
Send me a post — card drop me a line — stat - ing — point of view

— will you still be send-ing me a va - len - tine,
— you can knit a sweat-er by the fire - side,
— in - di -cate pre-cise-ly what you mean to say, —

Tacet . . . . ★

birth - day greet -ings, bot - tle of wine. — If I'd been out — till
Sun - day morn -ings, go for a ride. — do -ing the gar - den
yours sin - cere -ly wast-ing a - way. — Give me your an - swer

quar -ter to three — would you lock the door —
dig - ging the weeds — Who could ask for more —
fill in a form — Mine for ev - er more —

3rd Time to ⊕

Will you still need — me, will you still feed — me. when I'm six-ty

four. (Tacet 1st)
2nd. Ev'-ry sum-mer we can rent a cot-tage in the Isle of Wight

Oo _____

if it's not too dear.

You'll be old - der
(Ah
We shall scrimp and
(We shall scrimp and

too.
save
save)

Ah   And if you
Grand-child-ren

say   the   word
on   your   knee

I   could   stay   with
Ve - ra,   Chuck   and

you
Dave

⊕ Coda

-four.   (Ho!)

Printed and bound in Great Britain by
Caligraving Limited Thetford Norfolk

(NO90632) 10/98 (32117/32118)